THE BREAD MACHINE COOKBOOK FOR BEGINNERS

Adopt a Healthier Lifestyle with Your Bread Machine
Vegetable and Gluten-free Bread

DAN RIDOLFI

described herein. Additionally, the information in the following pages is intended only for informational purposes and should thus be thought of as universal. As befitting its nature, it is presented without assurance regarding its prolonged validity or interim quality. Trademarks that are mentioned are done without written consent and can in no way be considered an endorsement from the trademark holder.

Table of contents

Introduction

A bread machine is made up of a bread pan and paddles that are built-in and are placed in the middle of a multi-purpose oven that is small and manageable, as well. This small oven has a built-in micro-computer, which is what you use to operate the bread maker. There are different settings on a bread maker, depending on the type of bread you intend to bake. These settings include those for white bread, whole bread, French bread, as well as simple dough like those of pizzas. There is also an option of a timer on the bread maker to enable it to go on and off automatically even when you are not in the vicinity to operate it. Making bread is an almost primal activity, with the very physical kneading, careful supervision of the rising dough, and the deep satisfaction of serving piping hot bread to your family. It is also incredible that a few simple ingredients can produce such a wonderfully complex finished food. Bread is a delight and can seem like culinary magic. Yet, bread making is a skill that even many professional chefs do not master because it takes time (and well-developed biceps) to create loaves for service and to offer to clients. In most cases, you have to start at 3:00 a.m. to allow for the completion of all the bread-making steps, and many people do not have this sort of commitment or patience. A bread machine is the right choice if you want to make bread at home without wasting too much time.

Bread is an everyday staple. A food item we regularly purchase, buying store-bought bread is undoubtedly convenient. However, store-bought bread is packed with chemical additives, extra sugars, and salts to ensure longer shelf life. Store-bought includes emulsifiers and agents, but a Basic Bread recipe is made up of very few affordable ingredients, none of which include words that I even struggle pronouncing. And when you look at the bigger picture, you'll see you are better off baking your bread, especially with quite a convenient and useful tool, such as a bread machine. There are many pros to making bread at home, including the fact that it is far tastier than your standard, mass-produced bread. Buying your ingredients means you can manage all of what goes in the machine and provides you the opportunity of seeking the freshest ingredients. Home-baked bread always contains more nutrients, and for those who have allergies, baking your bread can help you manage what gets included versus trusting what a store-bought bread promises in terms of it being nut-free, dairy-free, or gluten-free. Outside of professional kitchens, most people in today's fast-paced world do not have time to make homemade bread, especially when many different types of bread can be purchased at almost every store. Yet, commercially made loaves are pale, insignificant versions of the rich, delicious bread you can create yourself with a handy bread machine. Even someone with the most hectic schedule in the world has 5 minutes to load a bread machine and set a timer to produce hot, fragrant bread that is ready to eat at the end of the day. Cutting the first slice of a new loaf—usually while it is too warm—never loses its magic, and the first bite is always sublime.

This book will give you a simple understanding of how ingredients combine to produce bread and which factors can create less-than-perfect results. You will be introduced to a collection of recipes that can be used, for the most part, in 1-lb., 1½-lb., and 2-lb. bread machines. These recipes can serve as your foundation for new bread experiences and allow you to experience all the fun of serving homemade bread to friends and family.

Tools for Machine Bread

The bread-making process is a combination of water, flour, yeast, salt, and other ingredients that are baked. The exact procedure includes combining ingredients until the mixture becomes a hard dough or paste, accompanied by shaping the dough into a loaf.

The goals of New Zealand's bread-making processes (mechanical dough growth, bulk fermentation, and no-time doughs) are to develop dough that will arise quickly and have the characteristics needed to make good bread for the customer.

Dough made by any directions: must be sufficiently extensible to make good bread to expand and relax as it grows. Good dough can be expanded if it expands when pulled. It must also be stretchy, that is, it must have the power to carry the gases produced as they arise, and it must be robust enough to hold its shape and cell structure.

Once mixed with water, 2 proteins in flour (gliadin and glutenin) form gluten. Gluten is what brings such special characteristics to flour. Gluten is necessary for the production of bread and affects the properties of dough stirring, kneading, and baking. It is very necessary to know to mix the ingredients when you first start baking bread.

Using the Machine

The bread maker is fairly easy to use. First, familiarize yourself with the settings. Again, the settings will vary depending on the brand and model of the machine you're using. Here's an example of the typical settings found in a bread maker:

Select Button

You will press the appropriate buttons to choose the kind of bread you're making. The recipes will indicate which setting you should choose. Each setting varies in processing time:

Bake—1 Hour

Use this setting in making jams or dough.

Dough—1 Hour and 30 Minutes

This setting is used to prepare doughs you'll bake in a conventional oven, such as pizza, specialty bread, and rolls.

Express Bake—1 Hour and 20 Minutes

The setting quickly bakes larger loaves of bread at a longer duration than the other express bake setting.

Express Bake—58 Minutes

Use this in making bread in less than an hour. This is similar to the quick bread setting in other brands of a bread maker.

Sweet—2 Hours and 50 Minutes

The setting is used for recipes that call for ingredients that need sufficient time to brown, such as proteins, fats, and sugar.

French—3 Hours and 50 Minutes

A longer time is needed to come up with a heartier crust. French bread recipes need a longer time to rise, knead, and bake.

Whole Wheat—3 Hours and 40 Minutes

This is used for recipes that use more than half Whole Wheat flour. It gives the dough a longer rise time.

Basic—3 Hours

This setting gives the best results and can be used with almost all kinds of bread recipes.

Crust Color Button

This setting lets you choose how you want your bread crust to be. L means light, P is medium, and H is dark. It also shows the cycle number. For example, Whole Wheat bread requires 2 cycles so the crust display will read 2H.

Display

The machine allows you to monitor the remaining time for kneading and baking the bread, the color setting of the crust, and the number of the bread setting cycle. The display also shows the remaining time before the bread is done. The timer starts after pressing the start/stop button.

Timer Set Buttons

If your machine has this feature, you can use it to delay the time when your bread begins baking. You can, for example, start it while you are sleeping so you have a fresh loaf for breakfast.

Start/Stop Button

Press this once when you are ready to start the bread-making process. Do not stop before the process is done or else the cycle will repeat from the start.

Bread Machine Cycle

Bread machines are a fantastic kitchen accessory to own.

These small compact wonders have many options and settings for baking an assortment of bread masterfully. Once you become familiar with your bread machine's settings, the chance to create and experiment is endless.

It is essential to know what each setting on your machine can deliver, making it easier to understand what function to use when it is time to bake your loaf. Being on a first-name basis with your bread machine will allow you to create flavorsome bread, making you wish that you had purchased the machine sooner!

Bread machines can come in 2 different varieties. Some brands hold specific settings that you cannot alter, so it is wise to follow the instruction manual when making different styles of bread to see which setting will be ideal.

Whereas some bread machines come with Basic settings with times and programming that you can alter. For instance, if you notice that the bread did not rise as you hoped for, you can extend the rising time.

Now, let me help you understand the various cycles and settings that you can find on your bread machine.

Basic Cycle

This setting is the most commonly used function of the bread machine, allowing you to create standard bread. This function generally runs for 3 to 4 hours, depending on the loaf size and style of bread. You can also use this setting when making bread using Whole Wheat flour.

Sweet Bread Cycle

This cycle, as the name suggests, is for bread that has higher sugar or fat content than standard bread. The setting is also used when ingredients such as cheese and eggs are used. This function allows the bread to bake at a lower temperature than other functions as the ingredients included may cause the crust to burn or darken in color.

Nut or Raisin Cycle

Though you can add ingredients such as nuts and dried fruit pieces into your pan, some machines tend to churn them too finely. The nut or raisin cycle is there to ensure that these ingredients stay relatively chunky, adding texture and sweetness to the bread. This function is ideal as it alerts the baker when it's time to add in the nuts or fruit pieces.

Whole Wheat Cycle

Whole wheat bread needs to be kneaded and churned longer than your standard loaves. That is why this cycle is perfect for bread that calls for this type of flour to be used. This function allows the bread to rise high enough and stops it from becoming too dense.

French Bread Cycle

The majority of the bread from the Mediterranean regions such as Italy or France comes out far better when using this function rather than the Basic cycle. Many French styled loaves of bread hold none to very little sugar. Bread from these regions needs a longer rising time and a lower and longer temperature. This is so that it can create the textures and crusts we have grown to love and savor.

Dough Cycle

This cycle is perfect for making pizza dough and dough used for making dinner rolls. The machine will mix and knead your ingredients, allowing you to then remove the dough, add your desired toppings or fillings, and then continue to bake them in your conventional oven. This saves you from having to knead the dough yourself and leaves little cleaning afterward, which is a big win for everyone.

Rapid Bake Cycle

This is for those who make use of quick rise yeast in their bread recipes. The rapid cycle can take anywhere between 30 minutes to 2 hours of the Basic Bread cycle, saving you plenty of time. Note that the Rapid Bake cycle does vary from machine to machine.

Cake or Quick Cycle

This cycle ideal for recipes that contain no yeast, such as cakes. This a primary cycle to consider when making the store-bought cake and bread mixes. The bread machine does not knead the ingredients together like the other cycles. All it does is mixes the ingredients and bakes them. This cycle and baking time can also vary from 1 machine to the other.

Jam Cycle

Though bread is delicious served fresh from the bread machine, there is nothing quite as enjoyable as a warm slice of bread served with warm strawberry jam, 1 of my simple pleasures in life!

A jam cycle on a bread machine is an absolute treat. Quick tip, remember to finely dice your fruit before adding it to the bread machine for the best results. You can have a fresh pot of jam ready within 1 hour.

Time-Bake or Delayed Cycle

This is a novel setting that some bread machines have. It allows you to add the ingredients into the bread machine, and then programs it to start baking at a time suited to you. This is a smart and useful function—thanks to it, there have been many days when the house has been awoken to the smell of fresh bread baking.

Word to the wise, bread that has milk or eggs as part of its ingredients should only be delayed for 1 to 2 hours to reduce issues with food-borne bacteria.

Crust Functionality

The crust functionality on bread machines allows the user to select their crust of choice when making bread. Generally, there are 3 settings for a crust: soft, medium, and dark. A soft crust is always great, paired with white bread varieties. If you prefer a crispier crust, then the medium and dark crusts will appeal to you. If your bread contains sweeteners, nuts, and grains, it may cause the bread to brown faster. Thus, a light crust setting is recommended.

Bread Machine Techniques

The processes that occur in a bread machine are not that different than those you use when making bread by hand. They are just less work and mess. The primary techniques used in making bread from a bread machine are:

Mixing and Resting

The ingredients are mixed together well and then allowed to rest before kneading.

Kneading

This technique creates long strands of gluten. Kneading squishes, stretches, turns, and presses the dough for 20 to 30 minutes, depending on the machine and setting.

First Rise

This is also called bulk fermentation. Yeast converts the sugar into alcohol, which provides flavor, and carbon dioxide, which provides structure as it inflates the gluten framework.

Stir Down (1 and 2)

The paddles rotate to bring the loaf down and redistribute the dough before the second and third rise.

Second and Third Rise

The second rise is about 15 minutes. At the end of the third rise, the loaf will almost double in size.

Baking

There will be 1 final growth spurt for the yeast in the dough in the first 5 minutes or so of the baking process, and the bread bakes into the finished loaf.

Main Ingredients

The ingredients needed for bread making are very simple: flour, yeast, salt, and liquid. Other ingredients add flavor, texture, and nutrition to your bread, such as sugar, fats, and eggs. The basic ingredients include:

Flour is the foundation of bread. The protein and gluten in flour form a ne2rk that traps the carbon dioxide and alcohol produced by the yeast. Flour also provides simple sugar to feed the yeast and it provides flavor, depending on the type of flour used in the recipe.

Yeast is a living organism that increases when the right amount of moisture, food, and heat is applied. Rapidly multiplying yeast gives off carbon dioxide and ethyl alcohol. When yeast is allowed to go through its life cycle completely, the finished bread is more flavorful. The best yeast for bread machines is bread machine yeast or active dry yeast, depending on your bread machine model.

Salt strengthens gluten and slows the rise of the bread by retarding the action of the yeast. A slower rise allows the flavors of the bread to develop better, and it will be less likely the bread will rise too much.

Liquid activates the yeast and dissolves the other ingredients. The most commonly used liquid is water, but ingredients such as milk can also be substituted. Bread made with water will have a crisper crust, but milk produces rich, tender bread that offers more nutrition and browns easier.

Oils and fats add flavor, create a tender texture, and help brown the crust. Bread made with fat stays fresh longer because moisture loss in the bread is slowed. This component can also inhibit gluten formation, so the bread does not rise as high.

Sugar is the source of food for the yeast. It also adds sweetness, tenderness, and color to the crust. Too much sugar can inhibit gluten growth or cause the dough to rise too much and collapse. Other sweeteners can replace sugar, such as honey, molasses, maple syrup, brown sugar, and corn syrup.

Eggs add protein, flavor, color, and a tender crust. Eggs contain an emulsifier, lecithin, which helps create a consistent texture, and a leavening agent, which helps the bread rise well.

Sourdough

Sourdough is starter-made yeasted bread—a fermented combination of water and flour producing lots of bread. It can still be preserved for a long period. With a chewy, soft center and large air bubbles, the consequent loaf has a substantial crust. It makes a grilled cheese from the BOMB.

The following sections highlight the correct order to put ingredients in the bread pan to bake perfect loaves of bread.

Water/Milk

All of the other Basic Bread ingredients, including flour, salt, and yeast, needs a liquid medium to do their respective tasks. Water is the most common liquid ingredient; milk, buttermilk, cream, and juice are some common substitutes.

The liquid is usually the first ingredient to be added to the bread pan. This is very important as it maintains the ideal texture of your bread. The liquid should not be cold; ensure that it is lukewarm (between 80 and 90°F) whenever possible.

Butter/Oil

Butter, oil, or fat is usually added after the liquid. This is what gives bread crust its attractive brown color and crispy texture. Do not use cold butter that has just been taken out of the refrigerator. You can either microwave it for a few seconds or keep it at room temperature until it gets soft.

Sugar/Honey (if Using)

Sweet ingredients such as honey, corn syrup, maple syrup, and sugar are usually added after the butter as they mix easily with water and butter. However, the sweetener can be added before the butter as well. Sugar, honey, etc. serve as a feeding medium for yeast, so fermentation is stronger with the addition of sweet ingredients.

Eggs (if Using)

Eggs need to be at room temperature before they are added to the bread pan. If the eggs are taken from the refrigerator, keep them outside at room temperature until they are no longer cold. They keep the crust tender and add protein and flavor to the bread.

Chilled Ingredients

If you are using any other ingredient that is kept chilled, such as cheese, milk, buttermilk, or cream, keep it outside at room temperature until it is no longer cold, or microwave it for a few seconds to warm it up.

Salt

Use table salt or non-iodized salt for better results. Salt that is high in iodine can hamper the activity of the yeast and create problems with fermentation. Furthermore, salt itself is a yeast inhibitor and should not be touching yeast directly; that is why salt and yeast are never added together or 1 after another.

Spices (if Using)

Spices such as cinnamon, nutmeg, and ginger are often used to add flavor to the bread. They may be added before or after the flour.

Flour

Flour is the primary ingredient for any bread recipe. It contains gluten (except for the gluten-free flours) and protein, and when the yeast produces alcohol and carbon dioxide, the gluten and protein trap the alcohol and carbon dioxide to initiate the bread-making process.

There are many different types of flours used for preparing different types of bread. Bread machine flour or white bread flour is the most common type as it is suitable for most bread recipes. It's so versatile because it contains an ideal proportion of protein for bread baking.

Usually, flour is stored at room temperature, but if you keep your flour in your fridge, allows it to warm up before using it.

Seeds (if Using)

If a recipe calls for adding seeds such as sunflower seeds or caraway seeds, these should be added after the flour. However, when 2 different flours are being used, it is best to add the seeds in between the flours for a better mix.

Yeast

Yeast is the ingredient responsible for initiating the vital bread-making process of fermentation. Yeast needs the right amount of heat, moisture, and liquid to grow and multiply. When yeast multiplies, it releases alcohol and carbon dioxide.

You can use active dry yeast or bread machine yeast (both will be available in local grocery stores). Cool, dry places are ideal to store yeast packs.

Yeast is added to the bread pan last, after the flour and other dry ingredients. (For certain a type of bread, like fruit and nut bread, yeast is technically not the last ingredient, as the fruits or nuts are added later by the machine. However, yeast is the last ingredient to be added before starting the bread machine.)

Gluten-Free Bread

1. Gluten-Free White Bread

Preparation time: 10 minutes

Cooking time: 25 minutes

Servings: 8

Ingredients:

- 2 cups white rice flour
- 1 cup potato starch
- ½ cup soy flour
- ½ cup cornstarch
- 1 tsp. vinegar
- 1 tsp. xanthan gum
- 1 tsp. instant yeast (bread yeast should be gluten-free, but always check)
- 1 ¼ cup buttermilk
- 3 eggs
- ¼ cup sugar or honey
- ¼ cup coconut or olive oil

Directions:

1. Place all ingredients in the Cuisinart bread pan in the liquid-dry-yeast layering.
2. Put the pan in the Cuisinart bread machine.

3. Select the Bake cycle. Choose Gluten Free. Press Start.
4. 5 minutes into the kneading process, pause the machine and check the firmness of the dough. Add more flour if necessary.
5. Resume and wait until the loaf is cooked.
6. The machine will start the keep warm mode after the bread is complete.
7. Allow it to stay in that mode for about 10 minutes before unplugging.
8. Remove the pan and let it cool down for about 10 minutes.

Nutrition:

- **Calories:** 151
- **Sodium:** 265 mg
- **Dietary Fiber:** 4.3 g
- **Fat:** 4.5 g
- **Carbs:** 27.2 g
- **Protein:** 3.5 g

2. Brown Rice Bread

Preparation time: 10 minutes

Cooking time: 25 minutes

Servings: 8

Ingredients:

- Brown rice flour
- 2 eggs
- 1 ¼ cup almond milk
- 1 tsp. vinegar
- ½ cup coconut oil
- 2 tbsp. sugar
- ½ tsp. salt
- 2 ¼ tsp. instant yeast

Directions:

1. Place all ingredients in the Cuisinart bread pan in the liquid-dry-yeast layering.
2. Put the pan in the Cuisinart bread machine.

3. Select the Bake cycle. Choose Gluten-free. Press Start.
4. 5 minutes into the kneading process, pause the machine, and check the consistency of the dough. Add more flour if necessary.
5. Resume and wait until the loaf is cooked.
6. The machine will start the keep warm mode after the bread is complete.
7. Make it stay in that mode for about 10 minutes before unplugging.
8. Remove the pan and let it cool down for about 10 minutes.

Nutrition:

- **Calories:** 151
- **Sodium:** 265 mg
- **Dietary Fiber:** 4.3 g
- **Fat:** 4.5 g
- **Carbs:** 27.2 g
- **Protein:** 3.5 g

3. Brown Rice and Cranberry Bread

Preparation time: 10 minutes

Cooking time: 25 minutes

Servings: 8

Ingredients:

- 3 eggs, beaten
- 1 tsp. white vinegar
- 3 tbsp. gluten-free oil
- 1 ½ cup lukewarm water
- 3 cups brown rice flour
- 1 tbsp. xanthan gum
- ¼ cup flaxseed meal
- 1 tsp. salt
- ¼ cup sugar
- ½ cup powdered milk
- 2/3 cup cranberries, dried and cut into bits
- 2 ¼ tsp. instant yeast (bread yeast should be gluten-free, but always check)

Directions:

1. Preparing the ingredients. Mix all the wet and the dry ingredients, except the yeast and cranberries, separately.
2. Place all ingredients in the Cuisinart bread pan in the liquid-dry-yeast layering.
3. Put the pan in the Cuisinart bread machine.

4. Load the cranberries in the automatic dispenser.
5. Select the Bake cycle. Choose Gluten-free. Press start and wait until the loaf is cooked.
6. The machine will start the keep warm mode after the bread is complete.
7. Let it stay in that mode for around 10 minutes before unplugging.
8. Remove the pan and let it cool down for about 10 minutes. Layer them in the bread machine, in the liquid-dry-yeast layering. Do not add the cranberries.

Nutrition:

- **Calories:** 151
- **Sodium:** 265 mg
- **Dietary Fiber:** 4.3 g
- **Fat:** 4.5 g
- **Carbs:** 27.2 g
- **Protein:** 3.5 g

4. Gluten-Free Peasant Bread

Preparation time: 10 minutes

Cooking time: 25 minutes

Servings: 8

Ingredients:

- 2 cups brown rice flour
- 1 cup potato starch
- 1 tbsp. xanthan gum
- 2 tbsp. sugar
- 2 tbsp. yeast (bread yeast should be gluten-free, but always check)
- 3 tbsp. vegetable oil
- 5 eggs
- 1 tsp. white vinegar

Directions:

1. Preparing the ingredients. Bloom the yeast in water with the sugar for 5 minutes.
2. Place all ingredients in the Cuisinart bread pan in the yeast-liquid-dry layering.
3. Put the pan in the Cuisinart bread machine.
4. Select the Bake cycle. Choose Gluten Free. Press start and stand by until the loaf is cooked.
5. The machine will start the keep warm mode after the bread is complete.

6. Let it stay in that mode for approximately 10 minutes before unplugging.
7. Remove the pan and let it cool down for about 10 minutes.

Nutrition:

- **Calories:** 151
- **Sodium:** 265 mg
- **Dietary Fiber:** 4.3 g
- **Fat:** 4.5 g
- **Carbs:** 27.2 g
- **Protein:** 3.5 g

5. Gluten-Free Hawaiian Loaf

Preparation time: 10 minutes

Cooking time: 25 minutes

Servings: 8

Ingredients:

- 4 cups gluten-free 4
- 1 tsp. xanthan gum
- 2 ½ tsp. (bread yeast should be gluten-free, but always check)
- ¼ cup white sugar
- ½ cup softened butter
- 1 egg, beaten
- 1 cup fresh pineapple juice, warm
- ½ tsp. salt
- 1 tsp. vanilla extract

Directions:

1. Place all ingredients in the Cuisinart bread pan in the liquid-dry-yeast layering.
2. Put the pan in the Cuisinart bread machine.
3. Select the Bake cycle. Choose Gluten Free. Press open and wait until the loaf is cooked.
4. The machine will start the keep warm mode after the bread is complete.
5. Let it stay in that mode for 10 minutes before unplugging.

6. Remove the pan and let it cool down for about 10 minutes.

Nutrition:

- **Calories:** 151
- **Sodium:** 265 mg
- **Dietary Fiber:** 4.3 g
- **Fat:** 4.5 g
- **Carbs:** 27.2 g
- **Protein:** 3.5 g

6. Vegan Gluten-Free Bread

Preparation time: 10 minutes

Cooking time: 25 minutes

Servings: 8

Ingredients:

- 1 cup almond flour
- 1 cup brown or white rice flour
- 2 tbsp. potato flour
- 4 tsp. baking powder
- ¼ tsp. baking soda
- 1 cup almond milk
- 1 tbsp. white vinegar

Directions:

1. Place all ingredients in the Cuisinart bread pan in the liquid-dry-yeast layering.

2. Put the pan in the Cuisinart bread machine.
3. Select the Bake cycle. Choose Gluten Free.
4. Press start and wait until the loaf is cooked.
5. The machine will start the keep warm mode after the bread is complete.
6. Let it stay in that mode for at least 10 minutes before unplugging.
7. Remove the pan and let it cool down for about 10 minutes.

Nutrition:

- **Calories:** 151
- **Sodium:** 265 mg
- **Dietary Fiber:** 4.3 g
- **Fat:** 4.5 g
- **Carbs:** 27.2 g
- **Protein:** 3.5 g

7. Gluten-Free Simple Sandwich Bread

Preparation time: 5 minutes

Cooking time: 60 minutes

Servings: 12

Ingredients:

- 1 ½ cups sorghum flour
- 1 cup tapioca starch or potato starch
- 1/3 cup gluten-free millet flour or gluten-free oat flour
- 2 tsp. xanthan gum
- 1 ¼ tsp. fine sea salt
- 2 ½ tsp. gluten-free yeast for bread machines
- 1 ¼ cups warm water
- 3 tbsp. extra virgin olive oil
- 1 tbsp. honey or raw agave nectar
- ½ tsp. mild rice vinegar or lemon juice
- 2 organic free-range eggs, beaten

Directions:

1. Blend the dry ingredients except for the yeast and set aside.
2. Add the liquid ingredients to the bread maker pan first, and then gently pour the mixed dry ingredients on top of the liquid.
3. Make a well in the center part of the dry ingredients and add the yeast.

4. Set for Rapid 1 hour 20 minutes, Medium crust color, and press Start.
5. In the end, put it on a cooling rack for 15 minutes before slicing to serve.

Nutrition:

- **Calories:** 137
- **Sodium:** 85 mg
- **Dietary Fiber:** 2.7 g
- **Fat:** 4.6 g
- **Carbs:** 22.1 g
- **Protein:** 2.4 g

8. Grain-Free Chia Bread

Preparation time: 5 minutes

Cooking time: 3 hours

Servings: 12

Ingredients:

- 1 cup warm water
- 3 large organic eggs, room temperature
- ¼ cup olive oil
- 1 tbsp. apple cider vinegar
- 1 cup gluten-free chia seeds, ground to flour
- 1 cup almond meal flour
- ½ cup potato starch
- ¼ cup coconut flour
- ¾ cup millet flour
- 1 tbsp. xanthan gum
- 1 ½ tsp. salt
- 2 tbsp. sugar
- 3 tbsp. nonfat dry milk
- 6 tsp. instant yeast

Directions:

1. Whisk wet ingredients together and place them in the bread maker pan.
2. Whisk dry ingredients, except yeast, together, and add on top of wet ingredients.
3. Make a well in the dry ingredients and add yeast.

4. Select the Whole Wheat cycle, light crust color, and press Start.
5. Allow cooling completely before serving.

Nutrition:

- **Calories:** 375
- **Sodium:** 462 mg
- **Dietary Fiber:** 22.3 g
- **Fat:** 18.3 g
- **Carbs:** 42 g
- **Protein:** 12.2 g

9. Gluten-Free Brown Bread

Preparation time: 5 minutes

Cooking time: 3 hours

Servings: 12

Ingredients:

- 2 large eggs, lightly beaten
- 1 ¾ cups warm water
- 3 tbsp. canola oil
- 1 cup brown rice flour
- ¾ cup oat flour
- ¼ cup tapioca starch
- 1 ¼ cups potato starch
- 1 ½ tsp. salt
- 2 tbsp. brown sugar
- 2 tbsp. gluten-free flaxseed meal

- ½ cup nonfat dry milk powder
- 2 ½ tsp. xanthan gum
- 3 tbsp. psyllium, whole husks
- 2 ½ tsp. gluten-free yeast for bread machines

Directions:

1. Add the eggs, water, and canola oil to the bread maker pan and stir until combined.
2. Whisk all of the dry ingredients except the yeast together in a large mixing bowl.
3. Add the dry ingredients on topmost of the wet ingredients.
4. Create a well in the center of the dry ingredients and add the yeast.
5. Set Gluten-Free cycle, Medium crust color, and then press Start.
6. When the bread is done, lay the pan on its side to cool before slicing to serve.

Nutrition:

- **Calories:** 201
- **Sodium:** 390 mg
- **Dietary Fiber:** 10.6 g
- **Fat:** 5.7 g
- **Carbs:** 35.5 g
- **Protein:** 5.1 g

10. Easy Gluten-Free, Dairy-Free Bread

Preparation time: 15 minutes

Cooking time: 2 hours and 10 minutes

Servings: 12

Ingredients:

- 1 ½ cups warm water
- 2 tsp. active dry yeast
- 2 tsp. sugar
- 2 eggs, room temperature
- 1 egg white, room temperature
- 1 ½ tbsp. apple cider vinegar
- 4 ½ tbsp. olive oil
- 3 1/3 cups multi-purpose gluten-free flour

Directions:

1. Start with adding the yeast and sugar to the water, then stir to mix in a large mixing bowl; set aside until foamy, about 8 to 10 minutes.
2. Whisk the 2 eggs and 1 egg white together in a separate mixing bowl and add to the bread maker's baking pan.
3. Pour apple cider vinegar and oil into the baking pan.
4. Add foamy yeast/water mixture to baking pan.
5. Add the multi-purpose gluten-free flour on top.
6. Set for Gluten-Free bread setting and Start.

7. Remove and invert the pan onto a cooling rack to remove the bread from the baking pan. Allow cooling completely before slicing to serve.

Nutrition:

- **Calories:** 241
- **Sodium:** 164 mg
- **Dietary Fiber:** 5.6 g
- **Fat:** 6.8 g
- **Carbs:** 41 g
- **Protein:** 4.5 g

11. Gluten-Free Sourdough Bread

Preparation time: 5 minutes

Cooking time: 3 hours

Servings: 12

Ingredients:

- 1 cup water
- 3 eggs
- ¾ cup ricotta cheese
- ¼ cup honey
- ¼ cup vegetable oil
- 1 tsp. cider vinegar
- ¾ cup gluten-free sourdough starter
- 2 cups white rice flour
- 2/3 cup potato starch
- 1/3 cup tapioca flour
- ½ cup dry milk powder
- 3 ½ tsp. xanthan gum
- 1 ½ tsp. salt

Directions:

1. Combine wet ingredients and pour into bread maker pan.
2. Mix dry ingredients in a large mixing bowl, and add on top of the wet ingredients.
3. Select the Gluten-Free cycle and press Start.

4. Remove the pan from the machine and allow the bread to remain in the pan for approximately 10 minutes.
5. Transfer to a cooling rack before slicing.

Nutrition:

- **Calories:** 299
- **Sodium:** 327 mg
- **Dietary Fiber:** 1.0 g
- **Fat:** 7.3 g
- **Carbs:** 46 g
- **Protein:** 5.2 g

12. Gluten-Free Crusty Boule Bread

Preparation time: 15 minutes

Cooking time: 3 hours

Servings: 12

Ingredients:

- 3 ¼ cups gluten-free flour mix
- 1 tbsp. active dry yeast
- 1 ½ tsp. kosher salt
- 1 tbsp. guar gum
- 1 1/3 cups warm water
- 2 large eggs, room temperature
- 2 tbsp. + 2 tsp. olive oil
- 1 tbsp. honey

Directions:

1. Combine all of the dry ingredients, do not include the yeast, in a large mixing bowl; set aside.
2. Mix the water, eggs, oil, and honey in a separate mixing bowl.
3. Pour the wet ingredients into the bread maker.
4. Add the dry ingredients on top of the wet ingredients.
5. Form a well in the center part of the dry ingredients and add the yeast.
6. Set to Gluten-Free setting and press Start.

7. Remove baked bread and allow it to cool completely. Hollow out and fill with soup or dip to use as a boule or slice for serving.

Nutrition:

- **Calories:** 480
- **Sodium:** 490 mg
- **Dietary Fiber:** 67.9 g
- **Fat:** 3.2 g
- **Carbs:** 103.9 g
- **Protein:** 2.4 g

13. Gluten-Free Potato Bread

Preparation time: 5 minutes

Cooking time: 3 hours

Servings: 12

Ingredients:

- 1 medium russet potato, baked, or mashed leftovers
- 2 packets gluten-free quick yeast
- 3 tbsp. honey
- ¾ cup warm almond milk
- 2 eggs, 1 egg white
- 3 2/3 cups almond flour
- ¾ cup tapioca flour
- 1 tsp. sea salt
- 1 tsp. dried chive
- 1 tbsp. apple cider vinegar
- ¼ cup olive oil

Directions:

1. Combine the entire dry ingredients, except the yeast, in a large mixing bowl; set aside.
2. Whisk together the milk, eggs, oil, apple cider, and honey in a separate mixing bowl.
3. Pour the wet ingredients into the bread maker.
4. Add the dry ingredients on top of the wet ingredients.
5. Produce a well in the dry ingredients and add the yeast.
6. Set to Gluten-Free bread setting, light crust color, and press Start.
7. Allow cooling completely before slicing.

Nutrition:

- **Calories:** 232
- **Sodium:** 173 mg
- **Dietary Fiber:** 6.3 g
- **Fat:** 13.2 g
- **Carbs:** 17.4 g
- **Protein:** 10.4 g

14. Sorghum Bread

Preparation time: 5 minutes

Cooking time: 3 hours

Servings: 12

Ingredients:

- 1 ½ cups sorghum flour
- ½ cup tapioca starch
- ½ cup brown rice flour
- 1 tsp. xanthan gum
- 1 tsp. guar gum
- 1/3 tsp. salt
- 3 tbsp. sugar
- 2 ¼ tsp. instant yeast
- 3 eggs (room temperature, lightly beaten)
- ¼ cup oil
- 1 ½ tsp. vinegar
- ¾–1 cup milk (105–115°F)

Directions:

1. Blend the dry ingredients in a bowl, not including the yeast.
2. Add the wet ingredients to the bread maker pan, and then add the dry ingredients on top.
3. Next is making a well in the center of the dry ingredients and add the yeast.

4. Set to Basic Bread cycle, light crust color, and press Start.
5. Remove and lay on its side to cool on a wire rack before serving.

Nutrition:

- **Calories:** 169
- **Sodium:** 151 mg
- **Dietary Fiber:** 2.5 g
- **Fat:** 6.3 g
- **Carbs:** 25.8 g
- **Protein:** 3.3 g

15. Paleo Bread

Preparation time: 10 minutes

Cooking time: 3 hours and 15 minutes

Servings: 16

Ingredients:

- 4 tbsp. chia seeds
- 1 tbsp. flax meal
- ¾ cup, + 1 tbsp. water
- ¼ cup coconut oil
- 3 eggs, room temperature
- ½ cup almond milk
- 1 tbsp. honey
- 2 cups almond flour
- 1 ¼ cups tapioca flour
- 1/3 cup coconut flour
- 1 tsp. salt
- ¼ cup flax meal
- 2 tsp. cream tartar
- 1 tsp. baking soda
- 2 tsp. active dry yeast

Directions:

1. Combine the chia seeds + a tbsp. of flax meal in a mixing bowl; stir in the water, and set aside.
2. Dissolve the coconut oil in a dish, and let it cool down to lukewarm.

3. Whisk in the eggs, almond milk, and honey.
4. Whisk in the chia seeds and flax meal gel and pour it into the bread maker pan.
5. Stir the almond flour, tapioca flour, coconut flour, salt, and ¼ cup of flax meal.
6. Whisk the cream of tartar and baking soda in a separate bowl and combine it with the other dry ingredients.
7. Put the dry ingredients into the bread machine.
8. Make a little well on top and add the yeast.
9. Start the machine on the Wheat cycle, Light or Medium crust color, and press Start.
10. Remove to cool completely before slicing to serve.

Nutrition:

- **Calories:** 190
- **Sodium:** 243 mg
- **Dietary Fiber:** 5.2 g
- **Fat:** 10.3 g
- **Carbs:** 20.4 g
- **Protein:** 4.5 g

16. Gluten-Free Oat and Honey Bread

Preparation time: 5 minutes

Cooking time: 3 hours

Servings: 12

Ingredients:

- 1 ¼ cups warm water
- 3 tbsp. honey
- 2 eggs
- 3 tbsp. butter, melted
- 1 ¼ cups gluten-free oats
- 1 ¼ cups brown rice flour
- ½ cup potato starch
- 2 tsp. xanthan gum
- 1 ½ tsp. sugar
- ¾ tsp. salt
- 1 ½ tbsp. active dry yeast

Directions:

1. Add ingredients in the order listed above, except for the yeast.
2. Then form a well in the center of the dry ingredients and add the yeast.
3. Select the Gluten-Free cycle, light crust color, and press Start.

4. Remove bread and allow the bread to cool on its side on a cooling rack for 20 minutes before slicing to serve.

Nutrition:

- **Calories:** 151
- **Sodium:** 265 mg
- **Dietary Fiber:** 4.3 g
- **Fat:** 4.5 g
- **Carbs:** 27.2 g
- **Protein:** 3.5 g

17. Gluten-Free Cinnamon Raisin Bread

Preparation time: 5 minutes

Cooking time: 3 hours

Servings: 12

Ingredients:

- ¾ cup almond milk
- 2 tbsp. flax meal
- 6 tbsp. warm water
- 1 ½ tsp. apple cider vinegar
- 2 tbsp. butter
- 1 ½ tbsp. honey
- 1 2/3 cups brown rice flour
- ¼ cup corn starch

- 2 tbsp. potato starch
- 1 ½ tsp. xanthan gum
- 1 tbsp. cinnamon
- ½ tsp. salt
- 1 tsp. active dry yeast
- ½ cup raisins

Directions:

1. Mix flax and water and let the mixture stand for 5 minutes.
2. Combine dry ingredients in a separate bowl, except for the yeast.
3. Add wet ingredients to the bread machine.
4. Add the dry mixture on top and make a well in the middle of the dry mix.
5. Add the yeast to the well.
6. Set to Gluten-Free, light crust color, and press Start.
7. After the first kneading and rise cycle, add raisins.
8. Remove to a cooling rack when baked and let cool for 15 minutes before slicing.

Nutrition:

- **Calories:** 192
- **Sodium:** 173 mg
- **Dietary Fiber:** 4.4 g
- **Fat:** 4.7 g
- **Carbs:** 38.2 g
- **Protein:** 2.7 g

Whole Wheat Bread

18. Whole Wheat Bread

Preparation time: 9 minutes

Cooking time: 4 hours

Servings: 12 slices

Ingredients:

- 1 cup Lukewarm water
- 1 tbsp. Olive oil
- 2 cups Whole wheat flour sifted
- ½ tsp Salt
- 1 Tbsp Soft brown sugar
- 2 tbsp Dried milk powder, skimmed
- Fast-acting, easy-blend dried yeast

Directions:

1. Add the water and olive oil to your machine, followed by half of the flour.
2. Now apply the salt, sugar, dried milk powder, and remaining flour.
3. Make a little well or dip at the top of the flour. Then carefully place the yeast into it, making sure it doesn't come into contact with any liquid.

4. Set the wholemeal or whole-wheat setting according to your machine's manual, and alter the crust setting to your particular liking.
5. Once baked, carefully remove the bowl from the machine and remove the loaf, placing it on a wire rack to cool. I prefer not to add any toppings to this particular loaf, but you can, of course, experiment and add whatever you want.
6. Once cool, remove the paddle; and, for the very best results, slice with a serrated bread knife. Enjoy!

Nutrition:

- **Calories:** 160
- **Carbs:** 30.1 g
- **Fat:** 3,1 g
- **Protein:** 5 g

19. Honey Whole-Wheat Bread

Preparation time: 10 minutes

Cooking time: 3 hours and 40 minutes

Servings: 8 slices

Ingredients:

- 2 cups Water at 90°F–100°F (320°C–370°C)
- 2 tbsp. Honey
- 1 tbsp. Melted butter, at room temperature
- ½ tsp Salt
- 2 cups Whole-wheat flour
- 1 tbsp Active dry yeast

Directions:

1. Place the ingredients in your bread machine follow the order of your manufacturer's suggestion.
2. Choose the Whole Wheat program, Light or Medium crust, and press Start.
3. Once baked, let the loaf cool for 10 minutes.
4. Gently wiggle the bucket to remove the loaf. Then transfer it onto a rack to cool.
5. Enjoy!

Nutrition:

- **Calories:** 101
- **Carbs:** 19 g
- **Fat:** 2 g
- **Protein:** 4 g

20. Whole Wheat Peanut Butter and Jelly Bread

Preparation time: 10 minutes

Cooking time: 3 hours

Servings: 12 slices

Ingredients:

- 2 cups of Water at 90°F–100°F (320°C–370°C)
- 2 tbsp. Smooth peanut butter
- 1 tbsp. Strawberry jelly (or any preferable jelly)
- 1 tbsp Vital wheat gluten
- ½ tsp Salt
- 1 tbsp. Baking soda
- ½ tsp Active dry yeast
- 1 tbsp. Baking powder
- 1 Light brown sugar
- 2 cups Whole wheat flour

Directions:

1. As you prep the bread machine pan, add the following in this particular order: water, jelly, salt, peanut butter, brown sugar, baking powder, baking soda, gluten, Whole Wheat flour, and yeast.
2. Choose 1 ½ Pound loaf, Medium crust, Wheat cycle, and then start the machine.
3. Once baked, place it on a rack to cool and then serve.

4. Enjoy!

Nutrition:

- **Calories:** 230
- **Carbs:** 39 g
- **Fat:** 6 g
- **Protein:** 9 g

21. Bread Machine Ezekiel Bread

Preparation time: 10 minutes

Cooking time: 3 hours

Servings: 12 slices

Ingredients:

- ¼ cups Whole wheat flour
- 2 cups Bread flour
- ¼ cup Spelled flour
- 1 tbsp. Honey
- 1 tbsp Millet
- 1 tbsp Olive oil
- 1 tbsp. Wheat germ
- 1 tbsp Dry kidney beans
- 1 tbsp Barley
- 1 tbsp Dry lentils
- 1 tbsp Bread machine yeast
- 1 tbsp Dry black beans
- 2 cup Water at 90°F (320°C)
- ½ tsp Salt

Directions:

1. Soak all beans and grains in separate bowls overnight.
2. Boil the black beans, dry kidney beans for about 1 hour, and then add lentils, millet, and barley. Next, boil for 15 minutes more.
3. Assemble boiled ingredients in a food processor and mix until mashed.
4. Spread water into the bread machine pan, add 2 tbsp. of olive oil and honey, and then add the flour, wheat germ. In 1 corner, add salt in another 1 yeast and Start the Dough cycle.
5. When the bread machine beeps, add the mash to the dough and press the Whole Wheat cycle. Enjoy!

Nutrition:

- **Calories:** 192
- **Carbs:** 31 g
- **Fat:** 5 g
- **Protein:** 6 g

22. Honey-Oat-Wheat Bread

Preparation time: 10 minutes

Cooking time: 3 hours and 45 minutes

Servings: 16 slices

Ingredients:

- Active dry yeast
- 2 tbsp Sugar
- 2 cup Water at 1100°F (450°C)
- 2 cup All-purpose flour
- ¼ cup Whole wheat flour
- 1 cup Rolled oats
- 1 tbsp Powdered milk
- ½ tsp Salt
- 2 tbsp Honey

- 2 tbsp Vegetable oil
- 1 tbsp Butter softened
- Cooking spray

Directions:

1. Place the following into the pan of a bread machine: yeast, sugar, and water. Let the yeast dissolve and foam for approximately 10 minutes. In the meantime, in a bowl, combine the all-purpose flour, powdered milk, Whole Wheat flour, salt, and rolled oats. Pour the butter, honey, and vegetable oil into the yeast mixture. Then add the flour mixture on top.
2. Choose the Dough cycle and then push the Start button. Let the bread machine fully finish the process, which spans approximately 1 ½ hour. Place the dough into a 9x5-inch loaf pan that's coated with cooking spray. Leave the bread to rise in a warm place for 1 hour.
3. Preheat the oven.
4. Bake for approximately 35 minutes in the warmed oven until the top turns golden brown.
5. Enjoy!

Nutrition:

- **Calories:** 281
- **Carbs:** 45 g
- **Fat:** 9 g • **Protein:** 6 g

23. Butter Up Bread

Preparation time: 10 minutes

Cooking time: 3 hours

Servings: 12 slices

Ingredients:

- 1 cup Bread flour
- 2 tbsp Margarine, melted
- 2 tbsp Buttermilk at 1100°F (450°C)
- 1 tbsp Sugar
- 1 tbsp Active dry yeast
- 2 Eggs, at room temperature
- ½ tsp Salt

Directions:

1. Prepare the bread machine pan by adding buttermilk, melted margarine, egg, salt, sugar, flour, and yeast in the order specified by your manufacturer.
2. Select Basic/White Setting and press Start.
3. Once baked, transfer onto wire racks to cool before slicing.
4. Enjoy!

Nutrition:

- **Calories:** 231
- **Carbs:** 36 g
- **Fat:** 6 g
- **Protein:** 8 g

24. Butter Honey Wheat Bread

Preparation time: 5 minutes

Cooking time: 3 hours and 45 minutes

Servings: 12 slices

Ingredients:

- 1 tbsp Buttermilk
- 2 tbsp Butter, melted
- 1 tbsp Honey
- 2 cups Bread flour
- ¼ cup Whole wheat flour
- ½ tsp Salt
- 1 tbsp Baking soda
- 1 tbs[Active dry yeast

Directions:

1. Put all ingredients into the bread machine, by the way recommended by the manufacturer.
2. In my case, liquids always go first.

3. Run the bread machine for a loaf (1 ½ lb.) on the Whole Wheat setting.
4. Once the baking process is done, transfer the baked bread to a wire rack and cool before slicing.
5. Enjoy!

Nutrition:

- **Calories:** 170
- **Carbs:** 27 g
- **Fat:** 6 g
- **Protein:** 3 g

25. Buttermilk Wheat Bread

Preparation time: 8 minutes

Cooking time: 4 hours and 30 minutes

Servings: 16 slices

Ingredients:

- 2 tbsp Buttermilk, at room temperature
- 1 cup White sugar
- 1 tbsp Olive oil
- ½ tsp Salt
- 1 tbsp Baking soda
- 2 cup Unbleached white flour
- ¼ cup Whole wheat flour
- Active dry yeast

Directions:

1. In the bread machine pan, measure all ingredients in the order the manufacturer recommends.
2. Set the machine to the Basic White Bread setting and press Start.
3. After a few minutes, add more buttermilk if the ingredients don't form a ball. If it's too loose, apply a handful of flour.
4. 1 baked, let the bread cool on a wire rack before slicing.
5. Enjoy!

Nutrition:

- **Calories:** 141
- **Carbs:** 26 g
- **Fat:** 2.5 g
- **Protein:** 5 g

26. Cracked Fit and Fat Bread

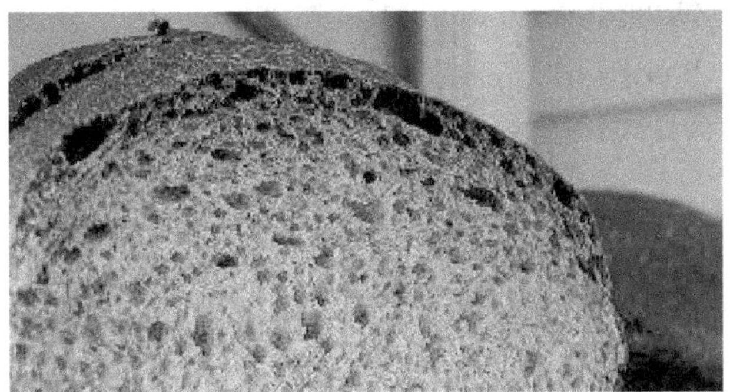

Preparation time: 5 minutes

Cooking time: 3 hours and 25 minutes

Servings: 16 slices

Ingredients:

- 1 cup Water
- 1 tbsp Butter softened
- 1 tbsp Brown sugar
- ½ tsp Salt
- ¼ cup Bread flour
- 1 cup Whole wheat flour
- 1 tbsp Cracked wheat
- 2 tbsp Active dry yeast

Directions:

1. In the bread machine pan, measure all components according to the manufacturer's suggested order.

2. Choose Basic/White cycle, Medium crust, and 2 lbs. weight of loaf, and then press Start.
3. Once baked, allow the bread to cool on a wire rack before slicing.
4. Enjoy!

Nutrition:

- **Calories:** 65
- **Carbs:** 12.4 g
- **Fat:** 1 g
- **Protein:** 2 g

27. Crunchy Honey Wheat Bread

Preparation time: 7 minutes

Cooking time: 3 hours and 30 minutes

Servings: 12 slices

Ingredients:

- 2 cup Warm water at 1100°F (450°C)
- 2 tbsp Vegetable oil
- 1 tbsp Honey
- ½ tsp Salt
- 1 cup Bread flour
- ¼ cup Whole wheat flour
- 1 tbsp Granola
- Active dry yeast

Directions:

1. Place the ingredients into the bread machine following the order recommended by the manufacturer.
2. Choose the Whole Wheat setting or the Dough cycle on the machine. Press the Start button.
3. Once the machine has finished the whole cycle of baking the bread in the oven, form the dough and add it into a loaf pan that's greased. Let it rise in volume in a warm place until it becomes double its size. Insert into the preheated 350°F (175°C) oven and bake for 35–45 minutes.

4. Enjoy!

Nutrition:

- **Calories:** 199
- **Carbs:** 37 g
- **Fat:** 4.2 g
- **Protein:** 6.2 g

28. Easy Home Base Wheat Bread

Preparation time: 10 minutes

Cooking time: 3 hours and 50 minutes

Servings: 12 slices

Ingredients:

- 2 cups Whole wheat flour
- ¼ cup Bread flour
- 1 tbsp Butter softened
- 1 cup Warm water at 900°F (320°C)
- 1 cup Warm milk at 900°F (320°C)
- Active dry yeast
- 2 Egg, at room temperature
- ½ tsp Salt
- 2 tbsp Honey

Directions:

1. Add the ingredients into the pan of the bread machine following the order suggested by the manufacturer.
2. Use the Whole Wheat cycle, choose the crust color, weight, and Start the machine.
3. Check how the dough is kneading after 5 minutes pass because you may need to add either 1 tbsp. of water or 1 tbsp. of flour-based on consistency.
4. When the bread is complete, cool it on a wire rack before slicing.
5. Enjoy!

Nutrition:

- **Calories:** 180
- **Carbs:** 33 g
- **Fat:** 2 g
- **Protein:** 7 g

29. Whole Wheat Yogurt Bread

Preparation time: 10 minutes

Cooking time: 3 hours and 40 minutes

Servings: 12 slices

Ingredients:

- 1 tbsp Ground nutmeg (optional)
- 2 cups Water
- 2 tbsp Butter, melted
- ¼ cup Plain yogurt
- 2 tbsp Dry milk
- 2 tbsp Honey
- 1 tbsp Active dry yeast
- 1 cup Whole wheat flour
- 1 cup Bread flour
- 2 tbsp Ground cinnamon
- ½ tsp Salt

Directions:

1. Begin by pouring ingredients into the bread pan in the instruction your manufacturer endorses. In my case, liquids always go first.
2. So, I begin with water, yogurt, butter, honey, sieve flour, dry milk, add salt, ground cinnamon, and yeast in different corners of the pan.
3. Select the Whole Grain setting, Light or Medium crust, and press Start.

4. When ready, allow it to cool and then serve.
5. Enjoy!

Nutrition:

- **Calories:** 158
- **Carbs:** 20 g
- **Fat:** 5 g
- **Protein:** 6 g

Vegetable Breads

30. Healthy Celery loaf

Preparation time: 2 hours 40 minutes

Cooking time: 50 minutes

Servings: 1 loaf

Difficulty: expert

Ingredients:

- 1 can (10 oz.) cream celery soup
- 1 tbsp. low-fat milk, heated
- 1 tbsp. vegetable oil
- 1¼ tsp. celery salt
- ¾ cup celery, fresh/sliced thin
- 1 tbsp. celery leaves, fresh, chopped
- 1 whole egg
- ¼ tsp. sugar
- ¼ cups bread flour
- ¼ tsp. ginger
- ½ cup quick-cooking oats
- 1 tbsp. gluten
- 1 tsp. celery seeds
- 1 pack active dry yeast

Directions:

1. Add all of the ingredients to your bread machine, carefully following the instructions of the manufacturer.
2. Set the program of your bread machine to Basic/White Bread and set crust type to Medium.
3. Press Start.
4. Wait until the cycle completes.
5. Once the loaf is ready, take the bucket out and let the loaf cool for 5 minutes.
6. Gently shake the bucket to remove the loaf.
7. Transfer to a cooling rack, slice, and serve.
8. Enjoy!

Nutrition:

- **Calories:** 73
- **Fat:** 4 g
- **Carbohydrates:** 8 g
- **Protein:** 3 g
- **Fiber:** 1 g

31. Broccoli and Cauliflower Bread

Preparation time: 2 hours 20 minutes

Cooking time: 50 minutes

Servings: 1 loaf

Difficulty: expert

Ingredients:

- ¼ cup water
- 1 tbsp. olive oil
- 1 egg white
- 1 tsp. lemon juice
- 2/3 cup grated cheddar cheese
- 1 tbsp. green onion
- ½ cup broccoli, chopped
- ½ cup cauliflower, chopped
- ½ tsp. lemon-pepper seasoning
- 2 cups bread flour
- 1 tsp. bread machine yeast

Directions:

1 Add all of the ingredients to your bread machine, carefully following the instructions of the manufacturer.
2 Set the program of your bread machine to Basic/White Bread and set crust type to Medium.
3 Press Start.
4 Wait until the cycle completes.
5 Once the loaf is ready, take the bucket out and let the loaf cool for 5 minutes.
6 Gently shake the bucket to remove the loaf.
7 Transfer to a cooling rack, slice, and serve.
8 Enjoy!

Nutrition:

- **Calories:** 156
- **Fat:** 8 g
- **Carbohydrates:** 17 g
- **Protein:** 5 g
- **Fiber:** 2 g

32. Zucchini Herbed Bread

Preparation time: 2 hours 20 minutes

Cooking time: 50 minutes

Servings: 1 loaf

Difficulty: intermediate

Ingredients:

- ½ cup water
- 1 tsp. honey
- 1 tbsp. oil
- ¾ cup zucchini, grated
- ¾ cup Whole Wheat flour
- ¼ cups bread flour
- 1 tbsp. fresh basil, chopped
- 1 tsp. sesame seeds
- 1 tsp. salt
- 1½ tsp. active dry yeast

Directions:

1. Add all of the ingredients to your bread machine, carefully following the instructions of the manufacturer.
2. Set the program of your bread machine to Basic/White Bread and set crust type to Medium.
3. Press Start.
4. Wait until the cycle completes.

5 Once the loaf is ready, take the bucket out and let the loaf cool for 5 minutes.
6 Gently shake the bucket to remove the loaf.
7 Transfer to a cooling rack, slice, and serve.
8 Enjoy!

Nutrition:

- **Calories:** 153
- **Fat:** 1 g
- **Carbohydrates:** 28 g
- **Protein:** 5 g
- **Fiber:** 2 g

33. Potato Bread

Preparation time: 3 hours

Cooking time: 45 minutes

Servings: 2 loaves

Difficulty: intermediate

Ingredients:

- 1 3⁄4 tsp. active dry yeast
- 1 tbsp. dry milk
- 1⁄4 cup instant potato flakes
- 1 tbsp. sugar
- 1⁄4 cups bread flour
- 1 1⁄4 tsp. salt
- 1 tbsp. butter
- 1 3/8 cups water

Directions:

1. Put all the liquid ingredients in the pan. Add all the dry ingredients, except the yeast. Form a shallow hole in the middle of the dry ingredients and place the yeast.
2. Secure the pan in the machine and close the lid. Choose the Basic setting and your desired color of the crust. Press Start.
3. Allow the bread to cool before slicing.

Nutrition:

- **Calories:** 35
- **Total Carbohydrate:** 19 g
- **Total Fat:** 0 g
- **Protein:** 4 g

34. Golden Potato Bread

Preparation time: 2 hours 50 minutes

Cooking time: 45 minutes

Servings: 2 loaves

Difficulty: expert

Ingredients:

- 1 tsp. bread machine yeast
- ¼ cups bread flour
- 1 ½ tsp. salt
- tbsp. potato starch
- 1 tbsp. dried chives
- tbsp. dry skim milk powder
- 1 tsp. sugar
- 1 tbsp. unsalted butter, cubed
- ¾ cup mashed potatoes
- 1 large egg, at room temperature
- ¾ cup potato cooking water, with a temperature of 80 to 90°F (26 to 32°C)

Directions:

1 Prepare the mashed potatoes. Peel the potatoes and put them in a saucepan. Pour enough cold water to cover them. Turn the heat to high and bring to a boil. Turn the heat to low and continue cooking the potatoes until tender. Transfer the cooked potatoes to a bowl and mash. Cover the bowl until the

potatoes are ready to use. Reserve cooking water and cook until it reaches the needed temperature.

2 Put the ingredients in the bread pan in this order: potato cooking water, egg, mashed potatoes, butter, sugar, milk, chives, potato starch, salt, flour, and yeast.
3 Place the pan in the machine and close the lid. Turn it on. Choose the Sweet setting and your preferred crust color. Start the cooking process.
4 Gently unmold the baked bread and leave it to cool on a wire rack.
5 Slice and serve.

Nutrition:

- **Calories:** 90
- **Total Carbohydrate:** 15 g
- **Total Fat:** 2 g
- **Protein:** 4 g

35. Onion Potato Bread

Preparation time: 1 hour 20 minutes

Cooking time: 45 minutes

Servings: 2 loaves

Difficulty: intermediate

Ingredients:

- 1 tbsp. quick-rise yeast
- ¼ cups bread flour
- 1 ½ tsp. seasoned salt
- tbsp. sugar
- 2/3 cup baked potatoes, mashed
- 1 ½ cup onions, minced
- 2 large eggs
- 2 tbsp. oil

- ¾ cup hot water, with a temperature 115 to 125°F (46 to 51°C)

Directions:

1. Put the liquid ingredients in the pan. Add the dry ingredients, except the yeast. Form a shallow well in the middle using your hand and put the yeast.
2. Place the pan in the machine, close the lid, and turn it on. Select the Express Bake 80 setting and Start the machine.
3. Once the bread is cooked, leave it on a wire rack for 20 minutes or until cooled.

Nutrition:

- **Calories:** 160
- **Total Carbohydrate:** 44 g
- **Total Fat:** 2 g
- **Protein:** 6 g

36. Spinach Bread

Preparation time: 2 hours 20 minutes

Cooking time: 40 minutes

Servings: 1 loaf

Difficulty: intermediate

Ingredients:

- 1 cup water
- 1 tbsp. vegetable oil
- ½ cup frozen chopped spinach, thawed and drained
- ¼ cups all-purpose flour
- ½ cup shredded Cheddar cheese
- 1 tsp. salt
- 1 tbsp. white sugar
- ½ tsp. ground black pepper
- ½ tsp. active dry yeast

Directions:

1 In the pan of the bread machine, put all ingredients according to the suggested order of manufacture. Set White Bread cycle.

Nutrition:

- **Calories:** 121
- **Total Carbohydrate:** 20.5 g
- **Cholesterol:** 4 mg
- **Total Fat:** 2.5 g
- **Protein:** 4 g
- **Sodium:** 184 mg

37. Curd Bread

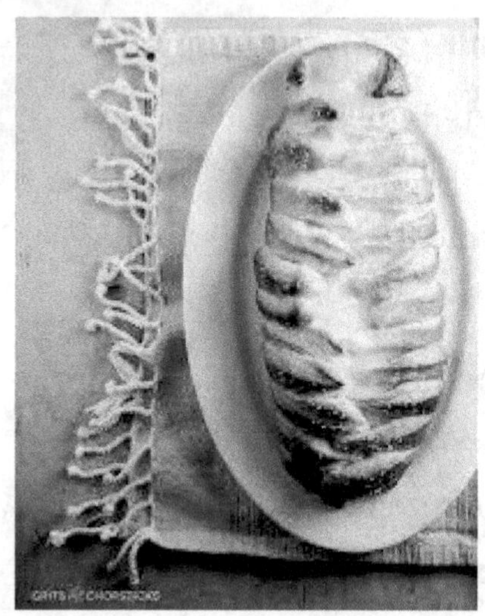

Preparation time: 4 hours

Cooking time: 15 minutes

Servings: 12

Difficulty: intermediate

Ingredients:

- ¾ cup lukewarm water
- 2/3 cups wheat bread machine flour
- ¾ cup cottage cheese
- 1 tbsp. softened butter
- 1 tbsp. white sugar
- 1½ tsp. sea salt
- 1½ tbsp. sesame seeds
- 1 tbsp. dried onions
- 1¼ tsp. bread machine yeast

Directions:

1. Place all the dry and liquid ingredients in the pan and follow the instructions for your bread machine.
2. Pay particular attention to measuring the ingredients. Use a measuring cup, measuring spoon, and kitchen scales to do so.
3. Set the baking program to Basic and the crust type to Medium.
4. If the dough is too dense or too wet, adjust the amount of flour and liquid in the recipe.
5. When the program has ended, take the pan out of the bread machine and let it cool for 5 minutes.
6. Shake the loaf out of the pan. If necessary, use a spatula.
7. Wrap the bread with a kitchen towel and set it aside for an hour. Otherwise, you can cool it on a wire rack.

Nutrition:

- **Calories:** 277
- **Total Carbohydrate:** 48.4 g
- **Cholesterol:** 9 g
- **Total Fat:** 4.7 g
- **Protein:** 9.4 g
- **Sodium:** 547 mg
- **Sugar:** 3.3 g

38. Curvy Carrot Bread

Preparation time: 2 hours

Cooking time: 15 minutes

Servings: 12

Difficulty: intermediate

Ingredients:

- ¾ cup milk, lukewarm
- 1 tbsp. butter, melted at room temperature
- 1 tbsp. honey
- ¾ tsp. ground nutmeg
- ½ tsp. salt
- 1 ½ cups shredded carrot
- ¼ cups white bread flour
- ¼ tsp. bread machine or active dry yeast

Directions:

1 Take 1 ½ lb. size loaf pan and first add the liquid ingredients and then add the dry ingredients.

2 Place the loaf pan in the machine and close its top lid.

3 Plug the bread machine into the power socket. For selecting a bread cycle, press Quick Bread/Rapid Bread, and for selecting a crust type, press Light or Medium.

4 Start the machine and it will start preparing the bread.

5 After the bread loaf is completed, open the lid and take out the loaf pan.

6 Allow the pan to cool down for 10–15 minutes on a wire rack. Gently shake the pan and remove the bread loaf.

7 Make slices and serve.

Nutrition:

- **Calories:** 142
- **Total Carbohydrate:** 32.2 g
- **Cholesterol:** 0 g
- **Total Fat:** 0.8 g
- **Protein:** 2.33 g

39. Potato Rosemary Bread

Preparation time: 3 hours

Cooking time: 30 minutes

Servings: 20

Difficulty: intermediate

Ingredients:

- 2 cups bread flour, sifted
- 1 tbsp. white sugar
- 1 tbsp. sunflower oil
- 1½ tsp. salt
- 1½ cups lukewarm water
- 1 tsp. active dry yeast
- 1 cup potatoes, mashed
- 1 tsp. crushed rosemary

Directions:

1. Prepare all of the ingredients for your bread and measuring means (a cup, a spoon, kitchen scales).
2. Carefully measure the ingredients into the pan, except the potato and rosemary.
3. Place all of the ingredients into the bread bucket in the right order, following the manual for your bread machine.
4. Close the cover.
5. Select the program of your bread machine to Bread with Fillings and choose the crust color to Medium.

6 Press Start.
7 After the signal, put the mashed potato and rosemary into the dough.
8 Wait until the program completes.
9 When done, take the bucket out and let it cool for 5–10 minutes.
10 Shake the loaf from the pan and let cool for 30 minutes on a cooling rack.
11 Slice, serve and enjoy the taste of fragrant homemade bread.

Nutrition:

- **Calories:** 106
- **Total Carbohydrate:** 21 g
- **Total Fat:** 1 g
- **Protein:** 2.9 g
- **Sodium:** 641 mg
- **Fiber:** 1 g
- **Sugar:** 0.8 g

40. Beetroot Prune Bread

Preparation time: 3 hours

Cooking time: 30 minutes

Servings: 20

Difficulty: intermediate

Ingredients:

- 1 ½ cups lukewarm beet broth
- 5 ¼ cups all-purpose flour
- 1 cup beet puree
- 1 cup prunes, chopped
- 1 tbsp. extra virgin olive oil
- 1 tbsp. dry cream
- 1 tbsp. brown sugar
- tsp. active dry yeast
- 1 tbsp. whole milk

- tsp. sea salt

Directions:

1 Prepare all of the ingredients for your bread and measuring means (a cup, a spoon, kitchen scales).
2 Carefully measure the ingredients into the pan, except the prunes.
3 Place all of the ingredients into the bread bucket in the right order, following the manual for your bread machine.
4 Close the cover.
5 Select the program of your bread machine to Basic and choose the crust color to Medium.
6 Press Start.
7 After the signal, put the prunes into the dough.
8 Wait until the program completes.
9 When done, take the bucket out and let it cool for 5–10 minutes.
10 Shake the loaf from the pan and let cool for 30 minutes on a cooling rack.
11 Slice, serve and enjoy the taste of fragrant homemade bread.

Nutrition:

- **Calories:** 443
- **Total Carbohydrate:** 81.1 g
- **Total Fat:** 8.2 g
- **Protein:** 9.9 g
- **Sodium:** 604 mg
- **Fiber:** 4.4 g
- **Sugar:** 11.7 g

41. Sun Vegetable Bread

Preparation time: 15 minutes

Cooking time: 3 hours 45 minutes

Servings: 8 slices

Ingredients:

- 2 cups (250 g) wheat flour
- 2 cups (250 g) whole-wheat flour
- 2 tsp. panifarin
- 2 tsp. yeast
- 1½ tsp. salt
- 1 tbsp. sugar
- 1 tbsp. paprika dried slices

- 2 tbsp. dried beets
- 1 tbsp. dried garlic
- 1½ cups water
- 1 tbsp. vegetable oil

Directions:

1. Set the baking program, which should be 4 hours; crust color is Medium.
2. Be sure to look at the kneading phase of the dough, to get a smooth and soft bun.

Nutrition:

- **Calories:** 253
- **Total Fat:** 2.6 g
- **Saturated Fat:** 0.5 g
- **Cholesterol:** 0 g
- **Sodium:** 444 mg
- **Total Carbohydrate:** 49.6 g
- **Dietary Fiber:** 2.6 g
- **Total Sugars:** 0.6 g
- **Protein:** 7.2 g

42. Tomato Onion Bread

Preparation time: 10 minutes

Cooking time: 3 hours 50 minutes

Servings: 12 slices

Ingredients:

- 2 cups all-purpose flour
- 1 cup wholemeal flour
- ½ cup warm water
- 4 ¾ oz. (140 ml) milk
- 3 tbsp. olive oil
- 2 tbsp. sugar
- 1 tsp. salt
- 2 tsp. dry yeast
- ½ tsp. baking powder
- 5 sun-dried tomatoes
- 1 onion
- ¼ tsp. black pepper

Directions:

1. Prepare all the necessary products. Finely chop the onion and sauté in a frying pan. Cut up the sun-dried tomatoes (10 halves).
2. Pour all liquid ingredients into the bowl; then cover with flour and put in the tomatoes and onions. Pour in the yeast and baking powder, without touching the liquid.

3. Select the baking mode and Start. You can choose the Bread with Additives program, and then the bread maker will knead the dough at low speeds.

Nutrition:

- **Calories:** 241
- **Total Fat:** 6.4 g
- **Saturated Fat:** 1.1 g
- **Cholesterol:** 1 g
- **Sodium:** 305 mg
- **Total Carbohydrate:** 40 g
- **Dietary Fiber:** 3.5 g
- **Total Sugars:** 6.8 g
- **Protein:** 6.7 g

43. Tomato Bread

Preparation time: 5 minutes

Cooking time: 3 hours 30 minutes

Servings: 8 slices

Ingredients:

- 3 tbsp. tomato paste
- 1½ cups (340 ml) water
- 4 1/3 cups (560 g) flour
- 1½ tbsp. vegetable oil
- 2 tsp. sugar
- 2 tsp. salt
- 1 ½ tsp. dry yeast
- ½ tsp. oregano, dried
- ½ tsp. ground sweet paprika

Directions:

1. Dilute the tomato paste in warm water. If you do not like the tomato flavor, reduce the amount of tomato paste, but putting less than 1 tbsp. does not make sense, because the color will fade.
2. Prepare the spices. I added a little more oregano as well as Provencal herbs to the oregano and paprika (this bread also begs for spices).
3. Sieve the flour to enrich it with oxygen. Add the spices to the flour and mix well.

4. Pour the vegetable oil into the bread maker container. Add the tomato/water mixture, sugar, salt, and then the flour with spices, and then the yeast.
5. Turn on the bread maker (the Basic program—I have the White Bread—the crust Medium).
6. After the end of the baking cycle, turn off the bread maker. Remove the bread container and take out the hot bread. Place it on the grate for cooling for 1 hour.

Nutrition:

- **Calories:** 281
- **Total Fat:** 3.3 g
- **Saturated Fat:** 0.6 g
- **Cholesterol:** 0 g
- **Sodium:** 590 mg
- **Total Carbohydrate:** 54.3 g
- **Dietary Fiber:** 2.4 g
- **Total Sugars:** 1.9 g
- **Protein:** 7.6 g

44. Curd Onion Bread with Sesame Seeds

Preparation time: 10 minutes

Cooking time: 3 hours 50 minutes

Servings: 8 slices

Ingredients:

- ¾ cup water
- 3 2/3 cups wheat flour
- ¾ cup cottage cheese
- 2 tbsp. softened butter
- 2 tbsp. sugar
- 1 ½ tsp. salt
- 1 ½ tbsp. sesame seeds
- 2 tbsp. dried onions
- 1 ¼ tsp. dry yeast

Directions:

1. Put the products in the bread maker according to its instructions. I have this order, presented with the ingredients.
2. Bake on the Basic program.

Nutrition:

- **Calories:** 277
- **Total Fat:** 4.7 g
- **Saturated Fat:** 2.3 g
- **Cholesterol:** 9 g
- **Sodium:** 547 mg
- **Total Carbohydrate:** 48.4 g
- **Dietary Fiber:** 1.9 g
- **Total Sugars:** 3.3 g
- **Protein:** 9.4 g

45. Squash Carrot Bread

Preparation time: 15 minutes

Cooking time: 3 hours 45 minutes

Servings: 8 slices

Ingredients:

- 1 small zucchini
- 1 baby carrot
- 1 cup whey
- 1 ½ cups (180 g) white wheat flour
- ¾ cup (100 g) Whole Wheat flour
- ¾ cup (100 g) rye flour
- 2 tbsp. vegetable oil
- 1 tsp. yeast, fresh
- 1 tsp. salt
- ½ tsp. sugar

Directions:

1. Cut/dice carrots and zucchini to about 8–10 mm (½ inch) in size.
2. In a frying pan, warm the vegetable oil and fry the vegetables over medium heat until soft. If desired, season the vegetables with salt and pepper.
3. Transfer the vegetables to a flat plate so that they cool down more quickly. While still hot, they cannot be added to the dough.
4. Now dissolve the yeast in the serum.
5. Send all kinds of flour, serum with yeast, as well as salt and sugar to the bakery.
6. Knead the dough in the Dough for the Rolls program.
7. At the very end of the batch, add the vegetables to the dough.
8. After adding vegetables, the dough will become moister. After the fermentation process, which will last about an hour before the doubling of the volume of the dough, shift it onto a thickly floured surface.
9. Turn into a loaf and put it in an oiled form.
10. Conceal the form using a food film and leave for 1 to 1 1/3 hours.
11. Preheat oven to 450°F and put bread in it.

12. Bake the bread for 15 minutes, and then gently remove it from the mold. Lay it on the grate and bake for 15–20 minutes more.

Nutrition:

- **Calories:** 220
- **Total Fat:** 4.3 g
- **Saturated Fat:** 0.8 g
- **Cholesterol:** 0 g
- **Sodium:** 313 mg
- **Total Carbohydrate:** 39.1 g
- **Dietary Fiber:** 4.1 g
- **Total Sugars:** 2.7 g
- **Protein:** 6.6 g

46. Zucchini and Berries loaf

•

Preparation time: 1 hour

Cooking time: 25 minutes

Servings: 8

Ingredients:

- 2 ¼ cups flour
- 3 eggs whisked lightly
- 1 2/3 cups sugar
- 2 tsp. vanilla
- ¾ cup vegetable oil
- ¾ tsp. baking powder
- pinch baking soda

- ¼ tsp. salt
- 2 tsp. cinnamon
- 1 ½ cup blueberries
- 1 ½ cup shredded zucchini

Directions:

1. Preparing the ingredients. Blend the dry and wet ingredients in 2 different bowls.
2. Place all ingredients, except the berries, in the bread pan in the liquid-dry-yeast-zucchini layering.
3. Put the pan in the Hamilton Beach bread machine.
4. Load the berries in the automatic dispenser.
5. Select the Bake cycle. Set to Rapid White bake for 1 hour. Press Start.
6. 5 minutes into the cycle, add the berries.
7. Wait until the loaf is cooked.
8. The machine will start the keep warm mode after the bread is complete.
9. Let it stay in that mode for 10 minutes before unplugging.
10. Remove the pan and let it cool down for about 10 minutes.

Nutrition:

- **Calories:** 277
- **Cholesterol:** 9 g
- **Carbohydrate:** 48.4 g
- **Sugars:** 3.3 g
- **Dietary Fiber:** 1.9 g
- **Protein:** 9.4 g

47. Yeasted Carrot Bread

Preparation time: 10 minutes

Cooking time: 25 minutes

Servings: 8

Ingredients:

- ¾ cup milk
- 3 tbsp. melted butter, cooled
- 1 tbsp. honey
- 1 ½ cups shredded carrot
- ¾ tsp. ground nutmeg
- ½ tsp. salt
- 3 cups white bread flour
- 2 ¼ tsp. dry yeast

Directions:

1. Preparing the ingredients. Place the ingredients in your Hamilton Beach bread machine.
2. Select the Bake cycle. Program the machine for Rapid Bread and press Start.
3. If the loaf is done, remove the bucket from the machine.
4. Let the loaf cool for 5 minutes.
5. Mildly shake the bucket to remove the loaf and try it out onto a rack to cool.

Nutrition:

- **Calories:** 277
- **Cholesterol:** 9 g
- **Carbohydrate:** 48.4 g
- **Dietary Fiber:** 1.9 g
- **Sugars:** 3.3 g
- **Protein:** 9.4 g

48. Zucchini Rye Bread

Preparation time: 10 minutes

Cooking time: 25 minutes

Servings: 8

Ingredients:

- 2 cups all-purpose or bread flour
- 2 ¾ cup rye flour
- 2 tbsp. cocoa powder
- ½ cup cornmeal
- 1 tbsp. instant yeast
- ¼ cup olive oil
- 3 tbsp. molasses or honey
- 1 ½ cup lukewarm water
- 1 tsp. salt
- 1 ½ cup zucchini, shredded

Directions:

1. Preparing the ingredients. Dry the shredded zucchini but placing it in a towel and wringing it to remove excess moisture.
2. Place all the ingredients in the liquid-zucchini-flour-yeast layering.
3. Put the pan in the Hamilton Beach bread machine.
4. Select the Bake cycle. Choose White bread and Medium crust.
5. Press start and wait until the loaf is cooked.
6. The machine will start the keep warm mode after the bread is complete.
7. Let it stay in that mode for nearly 10 minutes before unplugging.
8. Remove the pan and let it cool down for about 10 minutes

Nutrition:

- **Calories:** 277
- **Cholesterol:** 9 g
- **Carbohydrate:** 48.4 g
- **Dietary Fiber:** 1.9 g
- **Sugars:** 3.3 g
- **Protein:** 9.4 g

49. Savory Onion Bread

Preparation time: 10 minutes

Cooking time: 25 minutes

Servings: 8

Ingredients:

- 1 cup water, at 80°F to 90°F
- 3 tbsp. melted butter, cooled
- 1 ½ tbsp. sugar
- 11/8 tsp. salt
- 3 tbsp. dried minced onion
- 1 ½ tbsp. chopped fresh chives
- 3 cups white bread flour
- 1 tsp. bread machine or instant yeast

Directions:

1. Preparing the ingredients. Place the ingredients in your Hamilton Beach bread machine.
2. Select the Bake cycle. Program the machine for Whitbread, pick the Light or Medium crust, and press Start.
3. Remove the bucket from the machine.
4. Let the loaf cool for 5 minutes.
5. Gently shake the bucket and turn it out onto a rack to cool.

Nutrition:

- **Calories:** 277
- **Cholesterol:** 9 g
- **Carbohydrate:** 48.4 g
- **Dietary Fiber:** 1.9 g
- **Sugars:** 3.3 g
- **Protein:** 9.4 g

50.Bread Machine Sweet Potato Bread

Preparation Time: 15 Minutes

Cooking Time: 2 Hours

Servings: 10

Ingredients:

- 1/2 cup plus 2 tbsp. water
- 1 tsp. vanilla extract
- 1 cup plain mashed sweet potatoes
- 4 cups bread flour
- 1/4 tsp. of ground nutmeg and cinnamon
- 2 tbsp. butter
- 1/3 cup dark brown sugar
- 1 tsp. salt
- 2 tsp. active dry yeast
- 2 tbsp. dry milk powder
- Raisins or chopped pecans if desired

Directions:

1. Add all the ingredients according to the manufacturer's suggested order.
2. Set white bread setting, light crust.
3. If desired, add raisins or pecans when your bread machine beeps for additional ingredients.
4. Wait until baked, then slice and enjoy.

Nutrition:

- **Calories:** 130
- **Total Carbohydrate:** 18 g
- **Total Fat:** 7 g
- **Protein:** 1 g

CPSIA information can be obtained
at www.ICGtesting.com
Printed in the USA
BVHW091709250521
608095BV00004B/1270